M000190511

ANCIENT AFRICA

LIBYA

EGYPT

CONGO

KENYA

AUTHOR
Tanya Earls

ILLUSTRATOR
Hope Scott

This book belongs to

_____

To my beautiful daughter, Kyah.
You are worthy.
Continue being Love and Light.
Té Amo

Ancient Africa

Copyright ©2020 by Tanya Earls, All rights reserved.

No part of this publication may be reproduced, stored in a retrieval system or transmitted in any way by means, electronic, mechanical, photocopy, recording or otherwise without the prior permission of the author except as provided by USA copyright law.

ISBN: 978-1-09834-302-6

First published by BookBaby Publishing.

Ancient Africa

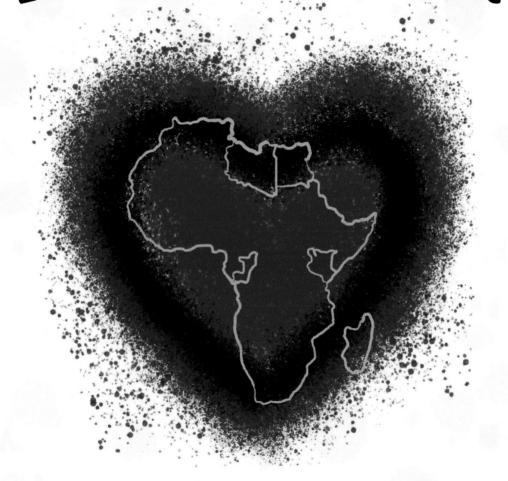

Tanya Earls

Once upon a time many,
many years ago in ancient Africa,
there existed some very fascinating
people and places.

Enkapune Ya Muto (Twilight Cave)
Kenya - around 40,000 years ago

Enkapune Ya Muto was an ancient workshop
and it is known as the Twilight Cave.

Can you guess what was made in the cave?

Inside this wondrous cave, ancient
Africans made shiny tools from jet-black
volcanic glass called obsidian. They
also made beautiful beads from ostrich
eggshells that were worn as jewelry.

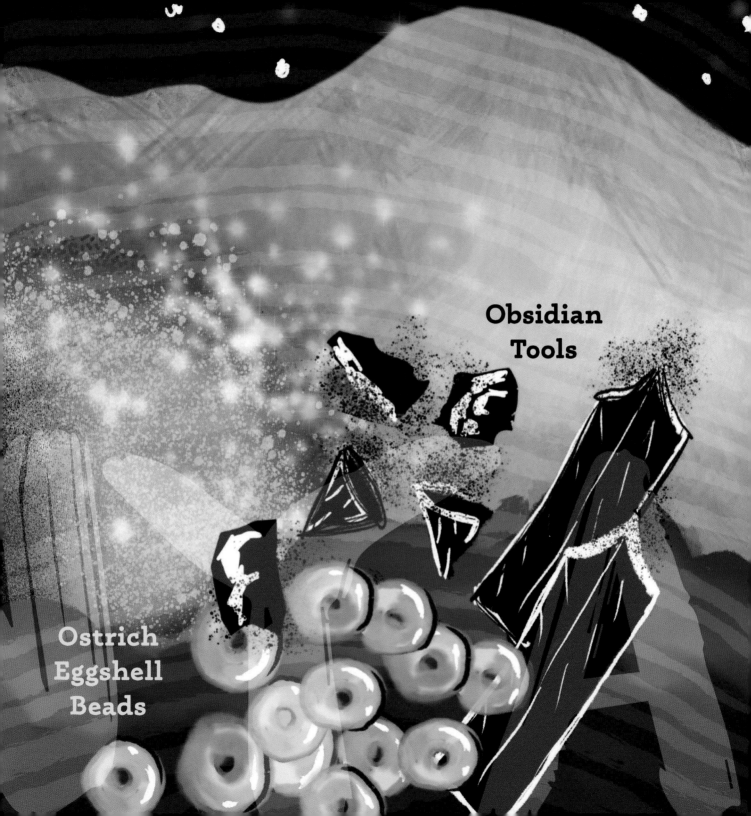

Ishango Bone
Congo - near the Semliki River,
around 20, 000 years ago

The Ishango Bone has one hundred sixty-eight "tally marks" thought to represent groups of numbers.

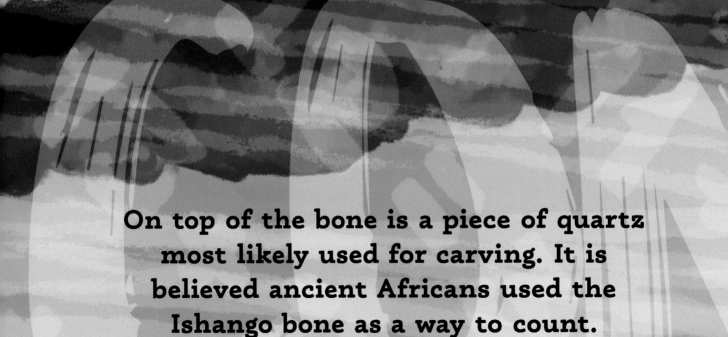

On top of the bone is a piece of quartz most likely used for carving. It is believed ancient Africans used the Ishango bone as a way to count.

Quartz

Is it possible
this rare bone
was used
for math?

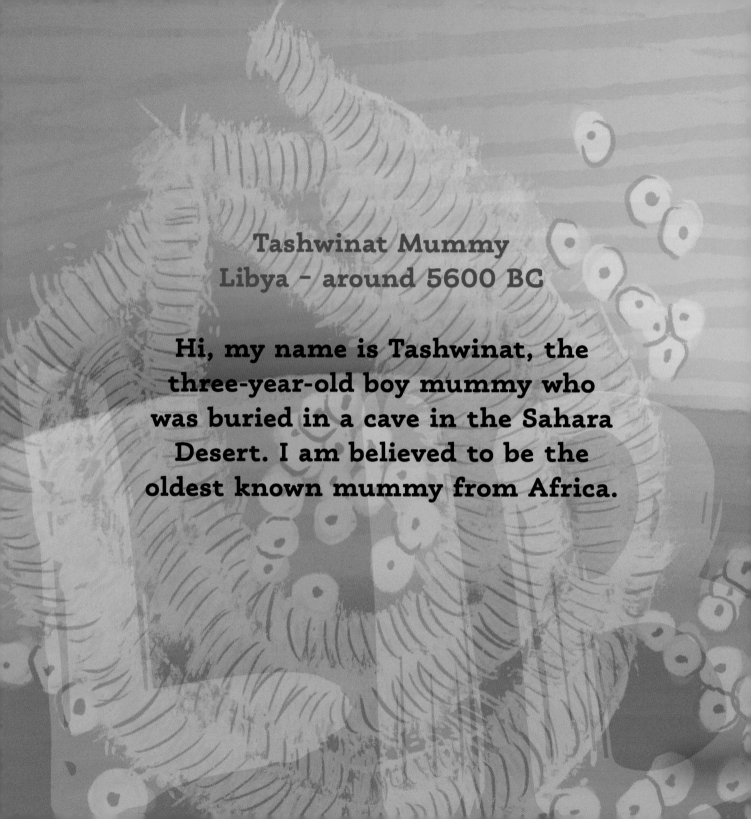

Tashwinat Mummy
Libya – around 5600 BC

Hi, my name is Tashwinat, the three-year-old boy mummy who was buried in a cave in the Sahara Desert. I am believed to be the oldest known mummy from Africa.

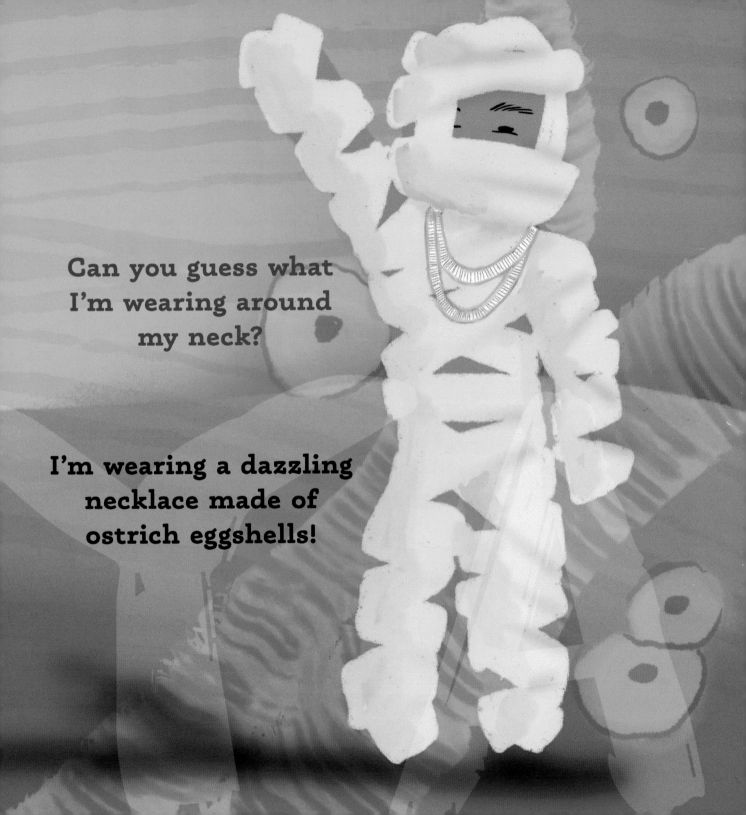

Nabta Playa (Stone Circle)
Egypt - Nubian Desert around 5500 BC

Nabta Playa is one of the oldest stone circles in the world.

Nabta Playa (Stone Circle)

It was used by ancient Africans as a way of timing the summer and winter seasons for growing food. The inner circle of stones is believed to have helped these ancient astronomers locate stars so they could travel in the dark.

Self-Discovery

As we embark down the road
Of generational recovery,
The first place to start
Is with self-discovery.

Happiness is found
As we solve our inner mystery.
Our connections strengthen
As we uncover hidden history.

May love always lead the way,
In the search for truth.
Each day leaves a new clue
To teach to our youth.

Marquise Payne

You are
AMAZING!

Can you help the giraffes make it to the Acacia tree?

Can you find?

Congo

Egypt

Libya

Kenya

AFRICA

LET'S

1   2

How many Ishango bones do you see?

COUNT!

How many Obsidian rocks?

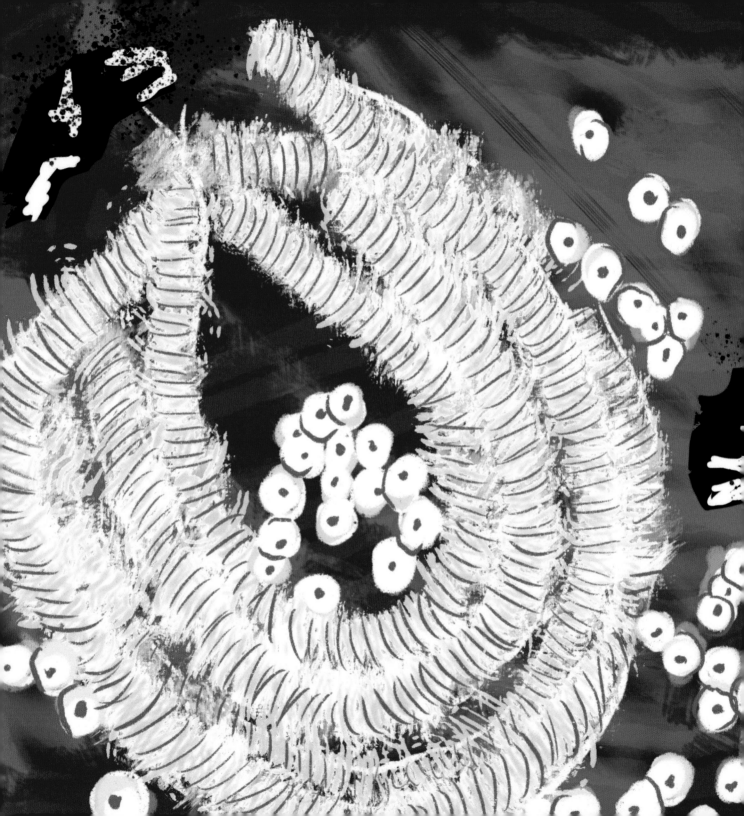

Tanya Earls is a nurse and mom to son, D'André and daughter, Kyah. She truly appreciates the arts and enjoys traveling. The beach is one of her favorite places. Tanya lives in the San Francisco Bay Area.